No One Home

Keith Westwater

No One Home

a boyhood memoir in letters and poems

KEITH WESTWATER

submarine

First published in 2018

Front cover image: Keith as a boy, Westwater family archives
Back cover image: Dome Valley Summit Track, Epic Little Missions

Cover design: Mākaro Press
Book design: Keith Westwater & Paul Stewart
Typesetting: Paul Stewart
Editor: Mary McCallum

ISBN 978-0-9951092-0-9

A catalogue record for this book is available from the National Library of New Zealand.

Printed by Wakefields Digital,
Wellington, New Zealand

submarine
imprint of Mākaro Press
PO Box 9321 Marion Square, Wellington 6141
makaropress.co.nz

The boy's family tree
has lost its heart.
The root is weak and sick.
Limbs tremble
in what's-coming winds.

To Avis Elaine

Contents

1938 Wedding Bells 13
1943 Letter to his sister 14
1948 Letter to her sister 19

1949–1956
To the North-lands

Wellsford 24
Wellsford Chronicle interview with the author 25
Brother 27
Roadside stop 28
Smoked fish and home brew 29
The paintings 31
Beaches 32
Before I knew it 33

1956–1957
To the Wasteland

Desert days 36
Three haiku 38

1957–1958
To South Auckland & Mount Roskill

Letter to the good stepmother 40
Learning to ride 42

Hansel and Hansel and the Widow Maw
Act I 44

Mount Roskill 45

Brief for the part of Maw 47

1958–1963
To Planet Maw

Maw's laws 50

School holiday bible camps 52

Playtime bullrush 54

The claws of Maw 55

Loaves and fishes 56

Hansel and Hansel and the Widow Maw
Act II 57

Intermediate days 58

Riding the news 60

The thrall of Maw 62

1963–1964
To the Gangplank

Hansel and Hansel and the Widow Maw
Act III 64

No one home 65

Foff and Babs and Hooke and me 66

Hansel and Hansel and the Widow Maw
Act IV 67

Letter from a recruitment officer 68
Why are you going? 69

Looking back

Conversations with a brother 74
Apologies 77
The ninetieth 78
Irreconcilable 79
Letter to a grandfather 80
To Avis Elaine 82

Epilogue 85

Acknowledgements 86

Cast

Avis Elaine	the boy's mother
Aunty Jean	Avis Elaine's sister
Wally	the boy's father
the boy	second son of Wally and Avis Elaine
brother	first son of Wally and Avis Elaine
Grandfather	Wally's father
Aunty Heather	Wally's sister
'Aunty' Jo	Avis Elaine's and Jean's stepmother, (the good stepmother)
Uncle Mike & Uncle John	Avis Elaine's half-brothers and Aunty Jo's twin sons
Maw	Wally's second wife (eventually), the boy's not-so-good and at times wicked stepmother
Old King Cole	*Auckland Star* newspaper agent
Foff, Babs, Hooke	school friends (the boy's tight trio)
Joy & Shorty	Foff's parents

1938
Wedding Bells

WESTWATER—LOGAN

St. David's Presbyterian Church, Auckland, was the scene of a pretty wedding of interest to Morrinsville on December 17, when the Rev. W. Bower Black officiated at the marriage of Miss Avis Elaine Logan, younger daughter of Mr. T. C. Logan, of Auckland, and the late Mrs Logan, to Mr. William Wallace Westwater, of Morrinsville, elder son of Mr. and Mrs. W. Westwater, of Hamilton.

The bride, who was escorted by her father, was attired in a Wedgwood blue ensemble with navy Bangkok straw hat and navy accessories. Her bouquet was of golden gladioli, roses and cornflowers.

Miss Jean Logan, who attended her sister, wore a frock of rose-coloured marocain, with halo hat to tone, and carried a bouquet of pink carnations, cornflowers and delphiniums.

Mr. R. B. Westwater, of Morrinsville, attended his brother as best man.

At the reception, which was held in the Parnell Tea Kiosk, the guests were received by Mrs. E. Colwell, friend of the bride. Mrs. Colwell wore a nigger brown floral frock and brown hat to match. Mrs. W. Westwater, mother of the bridegroom, chose a floral frock with wine-coloured background over which was worn a wine redingote, and her bouquet was of autumn-shaded dahlias and pansies.

When Mr. and Mrs. W. W. Westwater left on their honeymoon the bride travelled in an Air Force blue costume, navy halo hat and accessories to tone. Mr. and Mrs. Westwater are now residing in Morrinsville.

1943
Letter to his sister

ON ACTIVE SERVICE

NATIONAL PATRIOTIC FUND BOARD NEW ZEALAND

463725.
215th Comp. A.A. Barkey,
2. N.Z.E.F.
Date N.Z.A.P.O. 50.
4th March, 1943.

Dear Heather,

I am sitting on the edge of my bed with pad on knee, & candle for illumination — so please excuse bad writing. It is blowing a small gale outside & making valiant attempts to rain, but I feel very cosy inside the tent, especially as it has proved itself impervious to weather.

Your letter arrived safely, & I was very glad to hear from you again. To-day I received some "air-mail" — a letter from Avis, one from Mum & one from Dad (as well as the letter enclosed with Mum's), so I am as happy as a pup with two tails. Everybody here looks forward to mail-day, & I am no exception. Letters from home are a real blessing, & cheer us up no end.

Dad seems to have had a grand holiday at the

2.

NATIONAL PATRIOTIC FUND BOARD NEW ZEALAND

ON ACTIVE SERVICE.

Date.......................

mount & been very successful with his fishing. I wish I could say the same of my attempts at the latter. Perhaps I don't hold my mouth right.

Mum tells me that your bike is in action again, so you will be feeling pleased about that. I didn't feel very proud of my efforts at cycle riding the other day. These Army velocipedes are strange animals. There is no back pedal brake — only hand-brakes which act fore & aft — very suddenly when applied. I was blithely ignorant of their suddenness, but was very quickly enlightened when I found myself flying through the air over the handle-bars — like the man on the flying trapeze, though not so gracefully. Luckily I landed on a convenient patch of thick grass, & the only hurt I suffered was to my dignity. I now treat

3.

ON ACTIVE SERVICE.

Date.................................

Army bicycles with a great deal of respect.

Yesterday I had a game of cricket, & while batting a funny & mortifying experience happened — funny for the onlookers but mortifying for me. The bowler tossed the ball straight at my head, so naturally I ducked, & when it missed me I breathed a sigh of profound relief — which quickly changed to one of deep despair when I heard my wickets shattered. However, I had made 10 runs, so did not completely disgrace myself. I also had the questionable consolation of having provided amusement — & provoked loud laughter.

There are some very pretty shells on the beaches here, & I am trying to get a collection for you & Avis. So far my efforts have not been crowned with much success, as my

4.

NATIONAL PATRIOTIC FUND BOARD NEW ZEALAND

ON ACTIVE SERVICE.

Date

opportunities are fairly limited these days & the weather has not been of the best. I have not given up hope though, & will send you some as soon as I have enough.

During the past week or so the sea has been very rough, & on parts of the coast makes a marvellous sight as it dashes itself angrily against the rocks & high steep cliffs. I would like to take a photo of it, but feel sure that the result would fall far short of the reality. It is one of the wild savage moods of nature which needs to be actually seen to be enjoyed. The spectacle leaves you with a feeling of awe — & your thoughts turn to "the awful majesty of God", who created the oceans.

Please tell Dad that I still have plenty of malted milk left & do not need any more just now. It makes a great

5.

ON ACTIVE SERVICE.

NATIONAL PATRIOTIC
FUND BOARD
NEW ZEALAND

Date ....

drink these wet nights, just before turning in.

Well, Heather, I must close now. My regards to Mr. Brownlees, Mr. Butcher, Frank Mathers — & Mr. Henry.

Lots of love
from
Wallace.

XXXXX
XXXX
XXX

1948
Letter to her sister

4 Anderson Street,
Morrinsville.
2 November 1948

Dear Jean,
I thought I might have heard from you before this but you & Dad are both a couple of slow coaches, so I thought I'd write instead. You will probably receive a great surprise when you read my news but I'll have to tell you what is happening & has happened recently.

Wally has gotten into serious financial difficulties through gambling & our home is in the process of being sold & we are coming to Auckland to live as soon as possible. He will have to get a job & then look around for a roof for over our heads so if you hear of anything at all by way of a tent, shack or barn,

2

let us know immediately. Madge has offered to have me & the children until everything is settled & I won't be able to do much until after the baby arrives.

I saw the doctor on Saturday morning & he said that the baby might arrive any time within the next three weeks & it will be very small as I lost a lot of weight while I was sick. However I'm quite better again now & rapidly gaining again & will be glad when its all over.

Hows are you & Jim Dad & the children I hope you all well & will most likely see you early in the New Year. Wally's Mother came over today & she was asking after everybody. Dad was here on Friday fixing up with the solicitor about the whole business. They think they may be able to save the furniture but the house will be a complete loss & we will be without a penny. It's been an awful shock & I'll tell you all the details when I see you. Wally just about cracked up under the strain & has no doubt learnt his lesson.

I'll be pleased in a way to leave Morrinsville & come to Auckland although I wont like leaving some of my friends here. They all don't know about the position yet as I knew nothing myself until last Thursday & for quite a while refused to believe it was true. It wont come out in the papers as its all been settled out of court.

Well my dear my next letter will probably be far more cheerful as the worst is now over. So write soon & get Dad on the job too. It's ages since I heard from him, & I do

4

look forward to letters these days.

Give Malcolm & Carol a big hug each for me & our love to you all with a cheerio from your sister

Avis Elaine

From Precious to all XXXXXXXXXXX

1949–1956
To the North-lands

To find what I lost
when I had –
a mother and father,
a bucket
and spade.

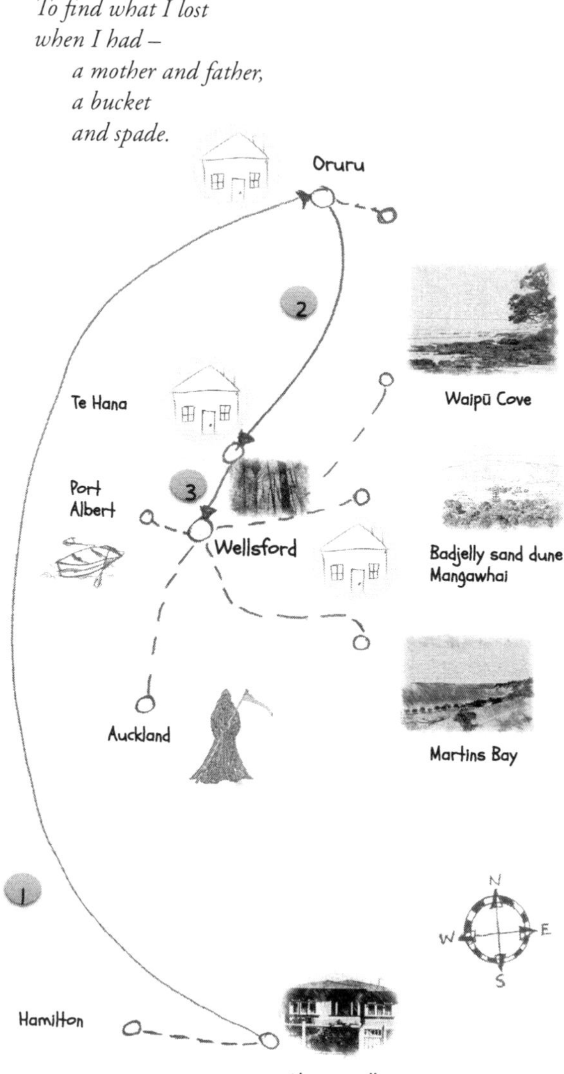

Wellsford

sticks, trees, rocks, stones
        old stumps, birds' bones
slimy stuff and mud
        to squish and squash
between our toes
        a track to slide down
on our bums, build a hut
        of ponga fronds –
bracken for a floor –
        make a dam of broken trees
or boat from twigs and leaves
        walk the plank, fly our flag
bury treasure in that cave
        (not *too* far in)
sail a raft of logs
        down the creek
lay a bridge, tickle eels
        catch tadpoles
pan for gold, have a swim
        before Mum calls us home

Wellsford Chronicle interview with the author

Interviewer I'd like to talk with you first about some of the pieces in *No One Home*, which, if it is to be taken literally, stitches together an almost Dickensian tale of you, I take it, as a boy and your fate – the fates – that befall you. The letter from the boy's mother to her sister and the one from his father to his sister – are they real or a bit of poetic licence?

Author Yes, both are genuine letters. The second was unearthed in Aunty Jean's possessions by her granddaughter about ten years ago, along with two earlier letters, and they haven't been embellished in any way.

Interviewer So, how soon after your mother's letter was written were you born, when did the family move – 'flee town' as it were – from Morrinsville, and where did you end up?

Author Well, I was born just under a week after the date on that letter. My relatives vary in their account of when we moved. I've gone with the 'three months later' version. I don't know if we spent any time in Auckland, as suggested in my mother's letter, but you will have read in 'Letter to a grandfather' that he found a job for Wally. This was as an accountant at a small dairy factory in a place called Oruru in the Far North.

Interviewer Mmm … I'm not sure there are many New Zealanders who have had the privilege of living there. And was it from Oruru to Wellsford, or was Wellsford the place of your first memories?

Author Yes, Wellsford is where my memories start. It's possible we lived in Mangōnui (now of fish and chip shop fame). We definitely lived in the small settlement of Te Hana just north of Wellsford prior to moving there …

Brother

'don't-touch' Meccano models
more marbles (in a bigger bag)
always taller (genes from
the lanky grandfather)

first read of next door's
Mickey Mouse and
Donald Duck comics
(the right of the eldest)

cutting his hand
with Dad's pocket knife
while making
a cotton-reel crawler

ignoring my wailing
to 'wait for me'
as he raced ahead
to the Saturday matinee

sprawled on the ground
chewing paspalum stalks
taking turns to name
shapes in the clouds

not knowing beside us
lay the ghost
of a sibling
they couldn't afford

Roadside stop

You were travelling by car?
Yes, a neighbour's perhaps.

Where were you going?
We were coming back.

Where had you been?
To a beach, no doubt.

Which one, do you know?
One south of home.

Why? Why not north?
We stopped on the way.

Tell me, where was that?
Probably the Dome Valley.

What happened then?
We entered the bush.

You think it was planned?
I'm sure – Dad had a spade.

What were you looking for?
A maidenhair fern, for her.

Smoked fish and home brew

Sometimes when I buy smoked fish and always when I watch *Foyle's War* (because Michael Kitchen looks just like you did, from wavy receding hair to short stature and 1940s suits), images appear from when I was small. Some are tangible – sepia photos taken with the family's Box Brownie in the 1950s. Others reside in my mind, but are as equally out of focus. Which may not matter.

Under our Wellsford house, propped up off the dirt floor, stood an old copper covered with a makeshift lid – a manufactury for your latest batch. It was surrounded by ingredients scattered on boxes and rudimentary shelves – hops, yeast, malt, sugar, each item in a pre-plastic packaging paradigm of paper bags, hessian sacks and cardboard packets. There was also apparatus, including rubber tubing through which, after sucking then spitting the first rush, you siphoned the brew into a queue of long-necked, quart-sized beer bottles, before arranging them in a wooden crate sitting by your feet. Pinching the tube between bottle-fills, you would, when finished, reach into a bag for a metal crown cap which you applied with a tap of a hammer and just enough pressure to make a seal, but not so much that the bottle would break. And me, five or six, having been admonished to watch not touch, and 'don't tell Mum you're here', looking on agog at the procedure, the craft, your concentration.

I guess you were doing this at times when you weren't off fishing on the Kaipara Harbour, probably at Port Albert. (How you got there, I'm not sure, as we didn't have a car; maybe there was a regular Railways bus and you caught one of those cream and blue-liveried under-powered coaches that lost a tooth off its gear wheels every time the driver double de-clutched, or maybe you teamed up with a mate who had a car.) In those days the Kaipara would have been teeming with snapper, mullet, gurnard, flounder, sole, and I'm sure it didn't take long to land a few in the bottom of the dinghy, the one I am perched in alongside you and my brother. If memory serves me right, I wasn't too keen on the boat thing at that age and squawked accordingly.

When you got home from fishing, you probably downed one of the six or so home-brew bottles now lined up on a shelf in our small wash house (we didn't have a fridge either). They and their replacements would slowly disappear on hot afternoons after you had been tending the vegetable garden, or on weekend evenings when your old army mates visited and the poker school got underway, or given as a thank you to the man who smoked your leftover catch.

The paintings

One day when I was six or seven
my brother showed me what was hidden
in the bottom drawer of Mum's dressing table
underneath the watercolours
she painted at the kitchen table
when we were in bed

I saw all the drawings
and watered-down-poster-paint,
stick-brush, stick-man
butcher-paper paintings
I'd painted at kindergarten
painted at school
painted for the tooth fairy

Beaches

What do you seek?
asks Waipū Cove.
        What's not in this
        beach-outing snap –
          rock pools
          a plastic ship
          wind in our hair.

What brought you here?
asks Martins Bay.
        The picnics we had
        on your shore –
          races in sacks
          egg-and-spoon
          three legs made from four.

What do you recall?
asks Mangawhai.
        A Badjelly sand dune
        that ate kids alive –
          the pipis we dug at low tide
          a Tilley lamp, Primus
          and tent.

Why do you still dig?
they all inquire.
        To find what I lost
        when I had –
          a mother and father,
          a bucket
          and spade.

Before I knew it

My brother and I are sitting at the table with Mum and Dad. Mum is talking to us and telling us that she has to go to hospital in Auckland to have an operation. Dad and she will be catching the bus down and my brother and I will be staying with the Robertsons. He is the local Presbyterian minister, and they live around the corner and down the road a bit.

I started asking why we couldn't come too and it didn't sound like much fun staying with the minister who always patted me too hard on the head after Sunday school. Mum said I would be fine and that they were very kind people and to be on my very best behaviour when we were staying there and that before I knew it she and Dad would be home again and we would be back in our own beds.

Shortly after that, we went to stay with the Robertsons. The only thing I remember about our stay is the telephone call. In the early hours of the morning of our second night, the phone rang and rang until there was a noise of clumping footsteps coming down the stairs. Within the fog of my sleep I became aware of one end of a long low-voiced conversation, then more clumping, going rapidly upstairs. After a short interval the minister's wife burst into the bedroom in which I was sleeping. She clutched me up, sobbing, and held me tightly.

'You poor boy, you poor, poor boy,' she wept, over and over.

1956–1957
To the Wasteland

The boy is asleep on a bus.
He wakes to see a mountain
with a necklace of lights.

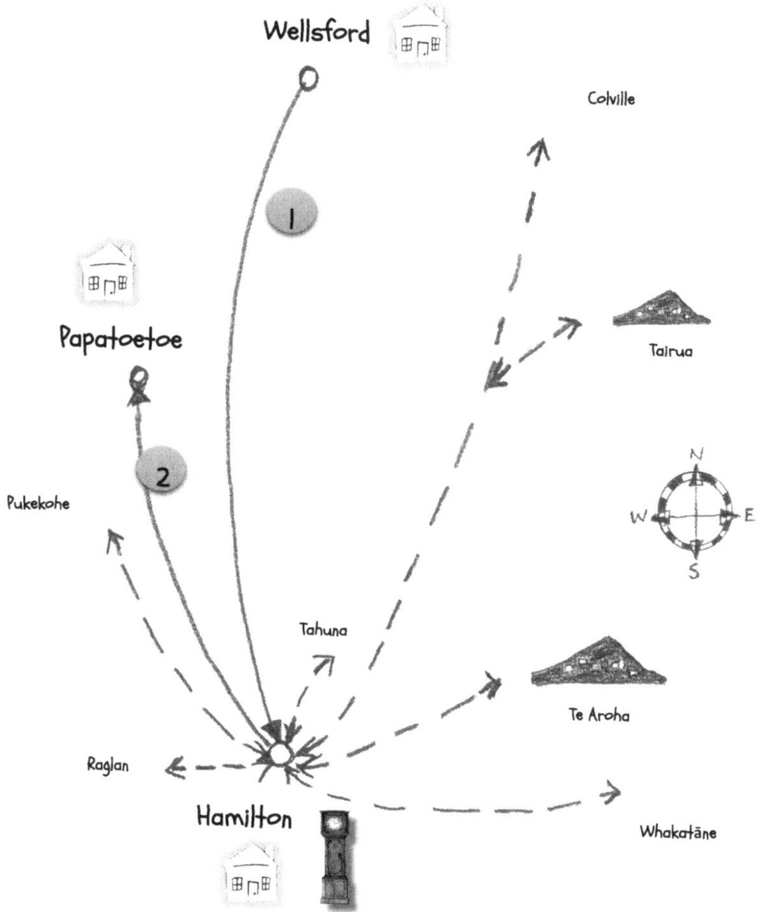

Desert days

The world is filled with remembering and forgetting / like sea and dry land. Sometimes memory / is the solid ground we stand on, / sometimes memory is the sea that covers all things / like the Flood. And forgetting is the dry land that saves … YEHUDA AMICHAI

Amnesia

He and his brother do not attend their mother's burial in Auckland, in keeping with the prevailing custom of protecting children from funerals and death. The boy knows his mother has died but he doesn't grieve the way grown-ups do. His way of coping is to behave badly and lock the cupboard on memories of his mother. He then loses the key where small boys lose things that make them feel sad.

The boy's family tree
has lost its heart.
The root is weak and sick.
Limbs tremble
in what's-coming winds.

Memories are made of this

When he is older, he is told that they lived on in Wellsford after his mother's death, that they had a housekeeper who was there when they came home from school, that she wasn't as nice as his mum, that the meals she prepared for them and their father weren't that great either. He is also informed that his father was offered a partnership at the accountancy firm in which he worked. But the firm's owner shone a due diligence torch on Wally's shady past and discovered that he was up to his old tricks again, so he was fired. The boy thinks they left Wellsford at the end of 1956 but can't be sure.

The boy and his brother
sing along to the song
Dean Martin is singing on the radio.
They stop when they see
their father crying.

Forty days and forty nights

He forgets where they went after that, but there were bus journeys and train journeys. There may have been several trips or one long trip with wayside stops. The boy remembers some places – a night or two (with a septic toe) in Pukekohe, a steam train taking on water at Frankton, their father teaching them to dog paddle in Whakatāne, staying on a dairy farm at Tahuna, and a long gravel-road bus trip (on which he suffered his usual motion sickness) up the Coromandel Peninsula to Colville. He wonders now whether his father was running away from or towards the bookies.

The boy is asleep on a bus.
He wakes to see a mountain
with a necklace of lights.
Was it Te Aroha –
or Tairua?

Three haiku

1.

Waiting forever
outside a pub –
Dad is booking his bets

2.

Grandparents' gas enamel oven
tick-tocking grandfather clock –
counting down our stay

3.

A new home
with Aunty Jo –
state house, Papatoetoe

1957–1958
To South Auckland & Mount Roskill

And he found a place to live
In a half-way house
Half-way down
Dominion Road

'Dominion Road'
— Don McGlashan

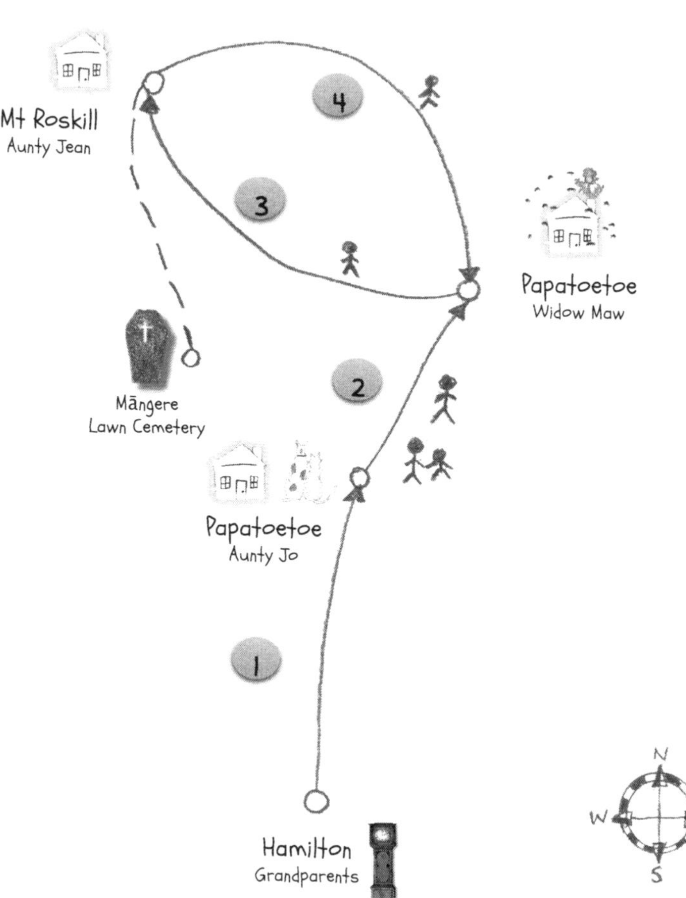

Letter to the good stepmother

Dear Aunty Jo

There were things Jean and Mike confided in me. Some were told when I was still young, staying at Jean's. She would ask me to sit next to her and she'd start talking about Avis. Other scraps of family history (or secrets) I didn't know until much later, well after you had died, when I pressed Mike and others.

I remember Mike and John's weddings in the 1950s. John's first, the one when Avis was still alive, and then Mike's. Were we living with you then? I know that I was resentful about shifting to a place I didn't know and you were going to be there too. Mike and John must have been in their late twenties, but I am now aware that you raised them mostly by yourself after Tom, my philandering grandfather, left you. So, here you were, a perennial parent, taking in Wally (an adult-child) and two of your non-bloodline grandchildren.

I whined that you were *old* and *stern* and *strict*, but was a little curious when I learnt that you had a cat and dog. They too would live with us at 42 Margaret Road – Tiki the tortoiseshell and Tūī the fox terrier. You worked as a cook at Middlemore Hospital. Early each morning you would walk to the Papatoetoe Station and return mid-afternoon and start cooking our tea. Sometimes you would bring home leftovers. I recall an apple pie and complaining on finding a surfeit of cloves in it. We couldn't have been easy, Wally, Murray, and I.

Years later, I asked Mike what the row was about that he and John had with Wally one evening. It had seemed pretty serious, with threats of Wally about to receive a hiding. Mike told me that he, John and you had given him money for a headstone for Avis. When nothing happened, they had him on. I had always supposed the ruckus was caused by Wally saying he was going to leave you and move us kids in with Maw (the mad axe-woman he met at the RSA). Not so. Wally, true to form, had gambled away the money for Avis's plaque.

You had your own fair share of sorrow (more than we ever knew – despite much research, Mike never could unearth your Welsh family of origin). Other than the grief from Avis dying, and Tom's antics, you suffered the loss of John after a cow kicked in his kidneys and they gradually gave up.

A long time later, we visited you as much as we could when you were living with your memories in Ōtara Court. Our kids were fascinated by your collection of silver souvenir teaspoons and you always gave them knitted dolls for presents.

Later still, addled with Alzheimer's, you would escape from the care home and walk for miles before they found you. We visited you just before you died. Mike warned us that you wouldn't know who we were. I still remember your eyes opening wide with astonishment when you saw me, followed by a smile of delight as you said my name.

With love

Learning to ride

Not long after my complaints
about the long walk to school

how everyone had one
so why couldn't I

you came home one night
with a two-wheeler bike –

a Monarch (boy's, second-hand)
front handbrake, rear pedal –

no bell, chain-guard or gears.
You bought it, no doubt

off a 'for sale' ad in the local rag
painted it fire-engine red

showed me how to use the pump
oil the chain, crank and hubs

told me to level the pedals
before I stood on one

straddled the cross bar
sat on the black saddle seat

while you palmed my back
steadied the handle bars

said to push with my feet –
one then the other – coaxed me

to steer straight, keep upright
as we practised setting off.

When I came a cropper
skinned my arms or knees

you painted them orange
set me up for another go

until I was able to wobble solo
up and down life's street.

If only that were so.

Hansel and Hansel and the Widow Maw
Act I

One day, two little brothers were taken on a walk by their father. Where are we going, Daddy? they asked and he replied, to a house I have found which is not in the Motherless Woods.

Why are we going to this house? they asked, and are Tiki and Tūī and Aunty Jo coming too? No, he replied, the house belongs to the Widow Maw and I am in her thrall. Then the brothers looked at each other and said why don't we lay a trail of crumbs in case we need to find our way back? Then they felt quite sad because they knew they had neither bread nor biscuits in their pockets.

So the little boys kept following their father but when they arrived at the Widow Maw's house a strange thing happened – their father shrivelled up and disappeared and when they looked around they were still deep, deep in the Motherless Woods and the house itself had a gorse hedge around it and stinging nettles growing in the window boxes and a scotch thistle for a chimney, and the Widow Maw, why, she had a wasps' nest on her head.

Mount Roskill

We didn't stay long when we first moved in with Maw, my brother and I. Rather, Maw insisted Dad farm us out while she shifted things round, drafted her rules, started scheming.

I was sent to Aunty Jean's in Dominion Road. It was nearer the intersection with Mt Albert Road than half-way down, but a half-way house, nevertheless. A rough-cast clad, semi-detached, two-up, two-down, early state house. A two-and-a-half bedroomed house, a house with a bathroom the size of a Morris Minor boot. A house inhabited by my slightly older cousins, Malcolm and Sally, chain-smoking Uncle Jim, who never spoke before lunch, and Aunty Jean, whose eyes went sad every time she looked at me.

How long was I there? Three, possibly six months. Long enough to be absent from my standard-three class photo at Papatoetoe West Primary School. My new, temporary school, Mt Roskill Primary, unlike my previous school, was full of street-smart kids and ancient desks with inkwells. I think I spent more time reading the graffiti and trying to make sense of the crude anatomical carvings on mine than learning anything I hadn't learnt already at Papatoetoe.

At the end of the school day I would walk home with Sally, sometimes stopping off at one of her friends on the way, but we always got to the house before her mother returned from her job as a seamstress at a nearby clothing factory. If Aunty Jean wanted Sally to run some errands (or even if she didn't), Sally would cadge some money for both of us to buy an ice-block or Coca-Cola at the dairy. My education in these matters was rounded off by Sally introducing me to creaming soda milkshakes and sherbets.

Malcolm, who was older than Sally, was chirpy, cheeky and often got into scrapes and trouble. When he did enough to rile his father, Uncle Jim would get the leather razor-strop he kept upstairs and lay into Malcolm with it. Afterwards Malcolm would retreat to his bedroom crying and whining. I soon learnt to steer clear of my uncle, though, strangely, I never feared he would do the same to me.

On the weekends, Sally and I would catch a bus to the Balmoral picture theatre and afterwards play at the nearby kids' playground. Jean and Jim would go to the workingmen's club and get tipsy. Sometimes flagons and crates of beer, friends and huge parcels of steaming fish and chips would assemble at their place or another's while we played or, when the women had consumed enough to indulge us, we would sample the Pimms, Blackberry Nip or sweet sherry dregs.

One evening, in the second week in April, Aunty Jean got me to sit on the couch beside her and asked me how much I remembered of my mum. Then she said why don't we catch the bus tomorrow and go and put some flowers on her grave. This we did, and although I didn't visit it again until thirty years later and the plot was still unmarked, I could remember exactly where it was in the large, sprawling Mangere Lawn Cemetery.

Not long after our trip to the burial ground, my stay at Aunty Jean's came to an end. Wally came to collect me and take me back to Papatoetoe. My life of living with Maw was about to commence.

Brief for the part of Maw

Eyes black as a Bandersnatch patch
eyebrows angled quertly back
hair dark brown, parmatier match
with a part, or pin in a festid bun

Thoughts as black as a Jubjub's hut
thin-lipped mouth derangier shut
slithering forth fomentious stuff
sputum, slime and frigilad fire

Heart as black as a manxome's byre
nose a roman mispalean pyre
no smiles gamsile or plamsy gyre
blouse and trou, no striffuled frocks

She prangles raths beneath the rocks
she trades in snakes and gimbles pox
with jaws that bite and claws that catch
she begat the Jabberwock.

1958–1963
To Planet Maw

Never, never talk to your father unless I say you can

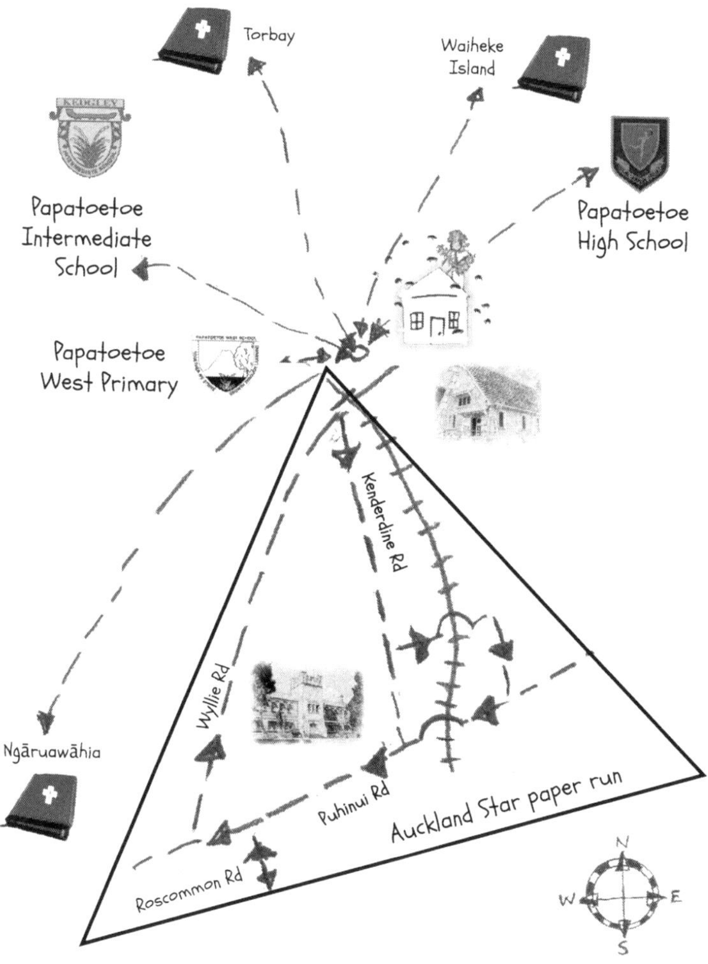

Maw's laws

1. Never use the front door

2. Before you come inside for the evening
   take off your shoes and clean and polish them
   leave them in the wash house
   then scrub your hands, arms and knees with the yellow soap

3. Each night, peel the vegetables

4. You will eat your tea in the kitchen
   not with your father and me
   then wash and dry the dishes after

5. You will go to your bedroom
   after you have done the dishes
   and not join your father and me in the lounge

6. You will go to church every Sunday – the Church of England just up the road and no other
   not the Presbyterian one where you were baptised
   nor the one your father took you to before you moved here
   neither your father nor I will come to church with you

7. You will stay after the service and go to Sunday school

8. You will attend catechism classes during the week –
   the ones taken by my brother-in-law, the Brigadier –
   and you will become confirmed

9. When you come home from school or your paper run you will stay outside
   until it's time to peel the vegetables

10. If it's raining, you can go to the bike shed, or the woodshed

11. Over the weekend you will do weeding
    under the shrubs and hedge
    and along the fence line

12. Don't touch the oleander's leaves – they are poisonous

13. Don't touch my collection of unwrapped linen
    in the linen cupboard

14. *Never, never* talk to your father unless I say you can

School holiday bible camps

Sat on a hill above the beach
Torbay was the first Maw sent us to.
After morning songs and scriptures
we would don togs, wrap rolled towels
round our necks, trek down the track
to the shore. The pastor suffered
small boys to sit on his knee.
One day we came back to find
the law leading him away.

The next was Waiheke Island –
C of E by the sea at Palm Beach
(or was it Onetangi?) and a curate
who ran like the devil was after him.
He trained with Peter Snell but chose
sack cloth and ashes over cinders.
We went there more than once –
had the fear of God put in us
should we miss the ferry back.

Last was west of Ngāruawāhia
run by an ex-rugby-playing cow cocky
with a Don Clarke haircut (All Black,
short all over). We ate, slept, washed
and were proselytised in the camp's
concrete block buildings that he built
after an epiphany on the road to Hamilton.
I supplicated him in vain to stay back
for one more week away from Maw.

We always found God, then forsook him
anywhere from a day to a month afterwards.
We took home books and brochures
marketing Christ. Maw let us keep them
for a week or two before she burnt them.

Playtime bullrush

Two captains
stood in the middle
took turns to call through
runners seeking a goal line
half a rugby field away.

First, the bulky and slow
who were easily caught
and stayed out there
as new chasers –
future tight forwards.

Last, the nifty and quick
who, like me, could weave
their way through
the throng untouched –
five-eights and wingers.

The claws of Maw

Here is the children's section. Try
The Chronicles of Narnia to start with –
I will tell you when you are allowed
to read it.

Now that I have seen your class photo
(and I can see that Leith is a Māori)
you will not go to play at his house
any more.

This grandfather clock belonged to your
grandfather. I am getting the plaque
removed that marks forty years of service –
it spoils it.

Today I was clearing out the wardrobe
and found some of your mother's
old paintings that your father had kept.
I burnt them.

Your father and I are getting married
in the registry office. There is only
room for my sons to come so you are
not invited.

I have bought you a bigger boy's bike.
Every Saturday you are to clean, oil
and polish it, then use it to get out
of my sight.

Loaves and fishes

Half a shilling bought
Friday's school lunch
steaming from the shop
newspaper wrapped

We sat cross-legged
on bare-boards floor
waiting for pieces of fish
and handfuls of chips

As we ate, our teacher
fed us nuggets of knowledge
reading out loud from
The Twelve Labours of Hercules

Hansel and Hansel and the Widow Maw
Act II

At night, the two little brothers were kept in a room by the Widow Maw. They weren't allowed out. Can we have some treacle pudding? they would ask, but Maw would just scowl and tell them to eat the tripe she had been boiling all afternoon.

During the day, the boys would follow the white pebble path to school, but on the way back the older brother would sometimes stray and play where Maw had forbidden him. Each time he came back to the house, Maw reached into her hair and set a wasp on him, which stung and stung until he cried. She would then hiss at the younger boy, telling him not to defy her or he too would get stung.

One day, the younger boy got back early and peeked inside a window. He saw the Widow Maw pedalling on a treadle grindstone, sharpening an axe. That night the small brothers opened their door just a little and could hear Maw talking on and on about the disobedient brother to a shadow that looked like their disappeared father. At the same time, she was chipping away with the axe at a limb of their family tree. They could read a name scratched on the limb.

Then the day the older brother turned fifteen, why the Widow Maw she snapped her fingers and the wasps drove him out of the house and he too disappeared. The younger brother was left to live in the house with the Widow Maw and the shadow of his father.

Intermediate days

A two-mile bike ride
with a mate or two.
Unlike Shakespeare's
whining schoolboy,
I raced there
eager for the day
and snail-paced home.

Two years, two teachers
whose names both began
with 'W' –
one an A-grade brain coach
the other nervous, earnest
unable to cope
with a class of forty
pubescent pre-teens.

Grey drill uniforms
though no marching
into classrooms
to martial music
like primary school.

The woodwork teacher,
drunk by the time
he got to work,
had breath more foul
than the evil glue
he heated on the stove.

We sniggered
when Norm and Carol
were caught playing
one-on-one games
down the far end
of the playing field.
Next day bans were read.

Riding the news

Down Kenderdine, my small-boy legs bowed and toes
just touching pedals, trying not to brake
too hard, lock-up, be thrown off with the weight,
trying to remember whether the next box
was a tube or slot, pick up time on the move
via a one-handed roll or further fold to fit,
not like runs that road-pitched at the front step.

Downhill, green canvas saddlebags
bulging with ninety inky newspapers,
other dailies rolled, rubber-banded, stacked
their rags in panniers fixed over
rear wheel carriers and in front-mounted
grocers' brown wicker delivery baskets,
not like my flat-folded, frame-straddled Stars.

Down Bridge Street, houses stopped by the railway line,
the gaoled bank robber's lifeless end-place,
standing shamed, yesterday's paper gone all the same,
dog-leg to Cambridge, then part-push, part-ride,
up the footbridge to run out the run on Puhinui with
a lap to where seal became gravel on Roscommon,
one last past the quarry, where houses turned to grass.

Downhill, home-gaol bound, light-biked, coat flapping,
glance to a road where we'd lived with Aunty Jo,
pedalling hard, looking but not looking at the stand-alone,
grey-stone orphanage, a reminder of Maw saying
to mind, or she will rid me there and I will have to wear
the drab-drill clothes all those sad-faced kids did –
like, she wouldn't really do that to me, would she?

The thrall of Maw

I paid your father's gambling debts
Thank me for my generosity
Your mother was a slut waitress

You are Wally's brats, feral pests
Better than my sons you will never be
I paid your father's gambling debts

I took you in, don't you forget
I take from his pay what he owes me
Your mother was a slut waitress

For an orphanage you were set
Your father – gaol, but for me
I paid your father's gambling debts

My first husband he cannot best
My son gave up his room for thee
Your mother was a slut waitress

You and your brother I detest
You're in my thrall eternally
I paid your father's gambling debts
Your mother was a slut waitress

1963–1964
To the Gangplank

because he liked going to school so much she would send him far away to a place where he could continue to do so. There he would also be paid and fed and clothed and shown lots of life and death skills

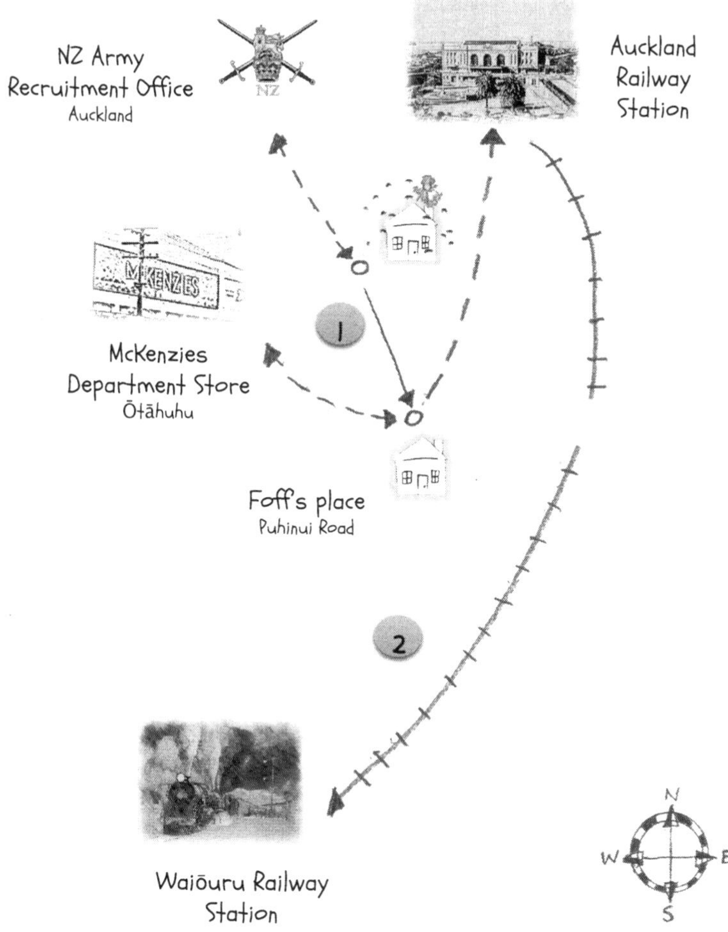

Hansel and Hansel and the Widow Maw
Act III

After the older brother disappeared, the younger brother was at first treated very nicely by the Widow Maw, who gave him cream buns and almost smiled. As he grew older, however, the wasps started getting buzzy with him. Also, he thought he could hear the sound of the treadle grindstone sharpening the axe again.

Over time, the wasps attacked more and more. Though the boy was very quick and did his best to avoid them, one or two would always get through and sting. All the while, the mute shadow of his father remained in thrall to Maw and did nothing to protect him.

So the boy grew sadder and sadder until he resolved to go to Old King Cole's place and ask if he could live with him and his family. And this he did, but although Old King Cole listened to the boy's request, he sent him back to live with Maw.

No one home

The boy he's flotsam on a lake
The boy he cannot sow or reap
The boy he's flayed by rage and hate
The boy he cries himself to sleep

And Maw she is a praying mantis
And Maw she's cut his father's hair
And Maw she's signed the dotted line
And Maw she's a lone press gang
And Maw she plots and cooks and schemes
And Maw she pries and lies and spies
And Maw she beats him with her words
And Maw she beats him with her stick
And Maw she's fit him up

The boy he is a small ball in a ruck
The boy he sups and eats alone
The boy he daily weaves and ducks
The boy he knows there's no one home

Foff and Babs and Hooke and me

We were tight for a while
the four of us fourth formers
indignant at Maw's malevolence

They had my back at school
kept score, shored me up
slaked my thirst for succour

Where are they, fifty years on?
Babs became an airline hostie
shifted to the Sunshine Coast

died ten years or so ago
Foff came a cropper
when his finance firm failed

following the GFC but
like stalwart Hooke always has
still calls and writes and visits

Hansel and Hansel and the Widow Maw Act IV

One day, the Widow Maw took him aside and hissed in his ear that she couldn't afford to keep him after year's end. But because he liked going to school so much she would send him far away to a place where he could continue to do so. There he would also be paid and fed and clothed and shown lots of life and death skills.

And the day the younger brother turned fifteen, why the Widow Maw she snapped her fingers, but this time the wasps, the house, the Widow Maw and the shadow of his father, they all disappeared! And the boy, he went off to live in the lee of the largest volcano in the land.

What happened there is another story.

Letter from a recruitment officer

1 August 1963

Dear Parent/Guardian,

I am pleased to inform you that your son/ward has been selected to enlist in the New Zealand Army as a Regular Force Cadet. His parent corps will be N.Z.A.E.C. and he has been provisionally accepted in the trade of A.E.W.S. N.C.O.

I note that your son/ward is currently aged fourteen but will be fifteen by the time he commences service. He will be required to spend three years as a R.F. Cadet and on completion of his Cadetship, he will graduate to his parent corps.

Your son/ward will be required to report for duty at Waiouru Military Camp on Monday 13 January 1964. Further information about what he is allowed to bring with him and tickets for his rail travel to the Camp will be sent to you in the near future.

Please sign the enclosed offer of service and return it to this office at your earliest convenience.

Yours faithfully,

New Zealand Army Recruitment Officer

Why are you going?

When the boy got to the platform at the Auckland railway station, it wasn't hard to work out who his fellow travellers were going to be. There were clumps of people standing by the red carriages. Teary mums, dads looking stoic, assorted relatives and friends doling out good wishes and last-minute goodbyes were all surrounding a pick-and-mix of boys waiting impatiently for the guard to tell them to board.

The boy's group comprised Foff and Foff's mum and dad, Joy and Shorty, who had driven him to the station from Papatoetoe. To his surprise, Aunty Jean and Aunty Jo were also there. They were not enthusiastic about his going and said things like 'This shouldn't be happening' and 'Why didn't Wally do something about this?' As he expected, Wally hadn't come to see him off. It was a late Sunday afternoon in mid-January 1964. The train he was boarding was the overnight express steam train from Auckland to Wellington but in the early morning he would disembark at Waiōuru Military Camp.

The aunties Jean and Jo had also made a surprise appearance about a month before. During Christmas week they came into the McKenzies department store in Ōtāhuhu to find him. He had been working there as a shop assistant since leaving school the day he turned fifteen.

At the time, he was staying at Foff's place. They had been friends since meeting up at intermediate school. Foff had a cheeky smile that interrupted a sometimes serious exterior and they used to ride to and from school together. Foff would wait outside the gate for him in the morning before they set out. When Foff's parents got a television set, the boy would go around and watch *Bonanza* and other programmes. Everybody – Foff's family, relatives, and friends – would crowd into their lounge to be entertained by 'the box'.

Joy and Shorty, after Foff had explained to them what was happening to the boy, took him in on his fifteenth birthday. They said it was fine for him to live there until he left for the army two months later.

Joy and Shorty owned an old house on a half-acre section. The boy earned part of his keep by helping with the lawn-mowing. Shorty had two lawn mowers – an old reel mower with a hand clutch and a four-stroke rotary mower. The boy knew nothing about motors – as far as he knew, his father had never owned a car – so 'mucking about with engines' was never part of his repertoire. The boy didn't think Shorty was too pleased when he seized the engine on the rotary mower one Saturday, even though all Shorty said was 'I didn't tell you about putting oil in it, did I.'

Foff's older brother had left home, but used to drop in most days after work to see his parents and have a cup of tea. Other relatives or friends would also call in for a cuppa. They would sit around the table and tell the day's stories, laughing and giggling at who had done – or not done – what, slapping their knees or the table, and every now and then pulling Joy's leg a treat. Joy would take it all and serve up more of her homebaking. Foff and the boy would scoff the chocolate caramel square and the delicious cheese custard.

The boy would ride from Foff's place to his work at the McKenzies store in Ōtāhuhu. He would arrive drenched by rain or at least dripping sweat. Luckily the wide display counters he served behind allowed a degree of physical separation from the customers.

He couldn't recall how Aunty Jean and Aunty Jo found out that he was joining the army. He might have rung Jean himself and talked to her, or Wally may have told one of them surreptitiously. When they came into McKenzies that day shortly before Christmas in 1963, they questioned him anxiously:

'Why are you going? What are you going to do there?' – the same questions his teachers had asked and latterly his boss at McKenzies, who wanted him to stay on and take up a trainee manager's programme.

The boy gave them all his stock answer, 'The army will let me keep going to school. I'm going to do my School Cert.'

Aunty Jean and Aunty Jo were cross that the boy had already left high school, so his answer seemed to counter that. But the boy knew they had concluded that this was all Maw's doing.

Just before they left the McKenzies store, Aunty Jo reached into her purse and produced a small package. She told the boy it was a combined Christmas present and going-away gift. He opened it on Christmas Day. Inside was something neither of his aunties could have afforded to put their hard-earned cash into buying – a Farmers Trading Company Swiss-made gold wristwatch with a leather strap. The boy remembered to thank them for it before clambering onto the carriage.

As the train pulled away from the station, he felt as though a guillotine was slicing off a part of his life. What he was heading for, though, just had to be better than what he was leaving behind.

Looking back

we all paid for your
prior painting by numbers,
when you took hay
from the firm's books
and fed an army of horses

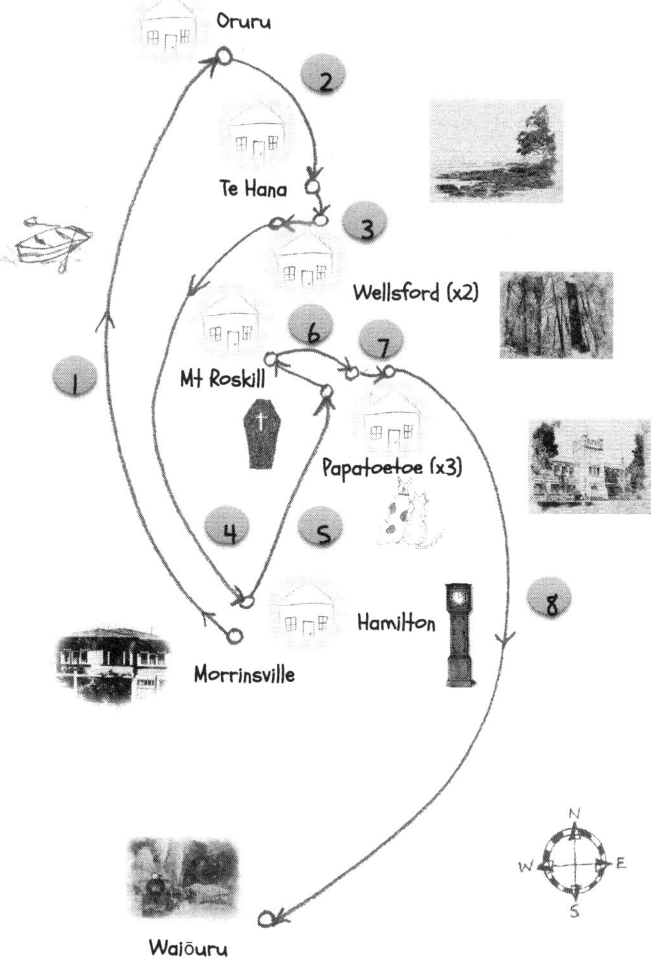

Conversations with a brother

I

brother What do you remember most about Dad? Do you remember he played cricket for a Wellsford team? And what about showing us how to play cribbage with matchsticks?

boy From when Mum was alive, not too much, really – probably not as much as you. I recall him meticulously putting stamps in his stamp albums, the ones that had gridded pages and a transparent insert between each leaf. I don't remember the cricket, but I do remember he played against a visiting Indian hockey side. He must have been about forty then and Mum was worried he was not fit enough. I can remember the cribbage and he also had a mahjong set. I don't think he ever hit us when we were kids.

II

brother What other things do you remember him doing with us?

boy You know, it's what Dad didn't do that comes most to mind, particularly after we went to live with Maw, as I now call her. You must have been about twelve and me nine. He didn't lift a finger when she started separating us off from him – and each other – or when she raged at us and hit us. And he didn't stop her schemes to get us out of the home when we both reached fifteen. I got really angry with him for that. I 'divorced' him in my head.

brother You can't have forgotten the cat fights she had with him?

boy Who could forget those? After you were packed off to Manurewa and I was still living with them, do you remember he used to arrange to see you some lunchtimes and not tell her? She found out through her spies, though, and gave him the usual hell.

III

boy Once when I was on leave from the army and staying at Aunty Jean's, she introduced me to a past drinking crony of Dad's. He looked at me with awe and said, 'You're Wally's boy? He's a hard man, your father.' People said at his funeral that he was a 'lovely' man, a 'gentle' man. To me, he was more like butter on a knife – soft and hard at the same time – but nothing in the middle.

brother Mmm … I wonder who that was. I didn't really see him as a 'hard' man.

IV

brother I've sent you a copy of Mum's death certificate and it wasn't cancer that killed her, as Jean seemed to say.

boy Thanks. It arrived today. I knew she had died in Greenlane Hospital. Yes, if you translate the certificate's medical language you can see it quite clearly – Avis died from a botched operation on her hiatus hernia. The surgeon bruised her heart. I remember Maw sometimes telling us – with a knowing look – that Mum died because Wally had broken her heart. I don't think she knew how close she was to the truth.

V

brother The plaque for Mum's grave that Mike and I organised is now in place. I got your share, thanks. I've put a photo in the mail.

boy Thanks for getting it sorted – I look forward to seeing it.

Apologies

Last night at the kebab shop, a slow boy
came up to me with a smile on his face
rubbed my arm several times before
his father came up and led him away

sorry, sorry, sorry, they said

It reminded me of the time my brother and I
visited you in hospital as you neared death
and you lay there, an old shrunken shadow
tears careering down your face

sorry, sorry, sorry, you said

I thought at last you were showing remorse
(as a judge might say) for your parental form
of Pontius Pilate care. Later I learnt that
stroke victims, no one knows why, often say

sorry, sorry, sorry, before they die

The ninetieth

We come in honour, Heather.
Your eyes twinkle – mirror to
humour, love, strength.

My cousins dry-rib you
like their father did,
kindle reminisences,

remark again on family
facsimiles – markers,
ties that bind,

my mum –
together times,
Dad away at war,

talk of stays and holidays
at Hukanui Road
and Whangamatā.

I recall a folding-in, making
room, being woven into
a real family's warp and weft.

Irreconcilable

to my father

A pair of small goldfinches
or chaffinches perhaps
painstakingly painted by numbers
accounting for time spent
in the ledger from leisure to death.
This cheaply framed token
is all I have of you
plus an unbalanced crockery set
your second wife said
was the entry for me in the will.
My preference was a photo of you
in World War Two –
3rd Division, Norfolk Island
rows of white tents
columns of Norfolk pines.
What would Avis have made
of your last pastiche?
Lost in jealous erasure
her countless watercolours
still gild my mind. The thing is,
we all paid for your
prior painting by numbers,
when you took hay
from the firm's books
and fed an army of horses.

Letter to a grandfather

Dear Bill

Gallipoli has been in the news recently, with the centenary of World War One. How old was my father when that started? Three, nearly four? And Heather, your only surviving child, now ninety, not even an afterthought.

They wrote, you may recall, he to her, when he was in the Solomons during World War Two. She gave me the letters some years ago, censor stamps all over the envelopes. He told her in closing he was her clever brother – must have been a family in-joke. Looking back, it isn't very funny, given what he did with his clients' money, being – like you – an accountant and all. Heather told me that you dipped deep into your retirement savings to repay those he'd defrauded, set him up with a new job far away, kept him out of the courts, never told Olive. And me just born.

I didn't really know you well enough to now address you with fondness and sadness. There are photos of you holding me aged three or four on the far-away front steps during a visit. We never lived close enough to you to grow close, and when Mum died early (surely from the stress of it all) you and Olive were too old to take us in for more than short stays.

I asked Heather one day whether you had gone to the war. She said that you tried to enlist but had flat feet (something you passed on to your great-grandson). So you never made it to Gallipoli, never faced Turkish fire at Anzac Cove or Chunuk Bair in that debacle of a campaign.

Our family history probably took the course it did because you didn't go to war. I can't imagine what would have happened had you not been around in 1948 to bail him out. Destitution and orphanages come to mind. Instead, my first seven years (the ones it is said that really matter for a child) stayed a 'normal' course.

I don't know whether my father ever expressed gratitude to you for what you did, but I will anyway – thank you, Bill, for doing the right thing by him and us.

You might be interested to know that I sometimes stay in Hamilton at the building you worked in for forty years – it's now an apartment-hotel. Your employers are still around but re-invented and just across the road. They are now called Fonterra.

In appreciation,

Your loving grandson

To Avis Elaine

The flowers you loved
        strew the shores
of my first seven years

Sometimes, in flower shops
        they shout out their names

        gerbera   gladioli   iris

Sometimes they sing to me
        from a bouquet
only half-made

        peonies   pansies   sweet pea

Sometimes they say all
        and nothing at all
the way flowers do

        cornflower   carnations   roses

Their scent is your shield of love
their leaves, the colour of your eyes
their petals, the clothes you clad me in

        as child and as man

Epilogue

Each of us harbors a homeland, a landscape we naturally comprehend. By understanding the dependability of place, we can anchor ourselves as trees — TERRY TEMPEST WILLIAMS

Your flood in me is the memory
of a northern whānau tree,
weak-rooted, whose heart
was killed and limbs lopped off
in acts not since accounted for.

Despite these things
that tree's terroir is in me
and I still long for
the streets, places, faces
of my youth
to be my home
to be my mother-land

and I still grieve for
possibilities which ceased to be
when the axe bit deep.

from 'River Talk'
— Keith Westwater

Acknowledgements

I wish to acknowledge the following for their assistance, input, or support: for passing to me the letters to the sisters, Aunty Heather and Sharon Tomoana (Aunty Jean's granddaughter); to my brother Murray, for the conversations we now have but never had growing up; to Elaine Bell and Paul Forsyth, for their lifelong friendship and understanding; to Jenny Clark, a former primary school classmate with whom I reconnected while completing this project and who sourced some of the photos I've used; and to Ti Kouka Café's Alice, Jesse and team, for once again providing me with a place to write (and excellent food and drink). I particularly wish to thank Margret Westwater for her patience, suggestions and advice, and Mary McCallum and Paul Stewart of Mākaro Press for making the publication of this work an enjoyable journey.

Versions of some of these poems have appeared in my blog *Some Place Else* and in the Interactive Publications anthology *Just Off Message*.

I am grateful for the use of the following:

(p.36) Excerpt from 'In My Life, On My Life' from *OPEN CLOSED OPEN: Poems* by Yehuda Amichai, translated from the Hebrew by Chana Bloch and Chana Kronfeld. Used by permission of Houghton Mifflin Harcourt Publishing Company. All rights reserved.

(p.39) Excerpt from 'Dominion Road'. Words and music by Don McGlashan. © Copyright Native Tongue Music Publishing Ltd. All print rights administered in Australia and New Zealand by Hal Leonard Australia Pty Ltd ABN 13 085 333 713 www.halleonard.com.au. Used By Permission. All Rights Reserved. Unauthorised Reproduction is Illegal.

(p.85) Excerpt from *An Unspoken Hunger: Stories from the Field* by Terry Tempest Williams, copyright ©1994. Used by permission of Brandt & Hochman Literary Agents, Inc. All rights reserved.

(p.88) Excerpt from 'Trouble With You'. Words and music by Don McGlashan.

(p.47) 'The brief for the part of Maw' references Lewis Carroll's nonsense poem 'Jabberwocky' from *Through the Looking-Glass.*

Permission has been granted for the use of the following images:
Dome Valley Summit Track, Epic Little Missions; Mangawhai Dune, creative commons photo by Steve; Wasp Swarm, Free-Stock-By-Wayne, deviantart.com, and thistle, Wikimedia Commons, drawing by Pearson Scott Foresman; Old Saint George's Church, Papatoetoe, Papatoetoe Historical Society; Wyllie Road Orphanage, Papatoetoe, Papatoetoe Historical Society; Auckland Railway Station c.1960, Wikimedia Commons, photo by Dennis Wilford; Waiōuru Railway Station, Grantham House Publishing, painting by WW Stewart; McKenzies department store sign, photographed by Morrie Hill, November 1956, ref 1/2-177164-F, Alexander Turnbull Library, adapted.

Some sketches by the author use the following images:
Overlooking Martins Bay, photo by Mike Parsons; Waipū Cove, photo by Lisa Ridings; grandfather clock, copyright-free drawing on ReusableArt.com. Crests for Kedgley Intermediate School (formerly Papatoetoe Intermediate School), Papatoetoe West Primary School and the New Zealand Army were sourced from those organisations' websites, and the crest for Papatoetoe High is from the school's 1963 magazine.

All other photos, sketches, maps, and map elements are from or by the author © Keith Westwater.

Me, I'd like to stand in the rain
Feel it washing me down
Find some place I can stand
Forever, ever, on and on

'Trouble With You'
— Don McGlashan